EXPLORING THE STATES

IOWA

THE HAWKEYE STATE

by Pat Ryan

BELLWETHER MEDIA • MINNEAPOLIS, MN

Note to Librarians, Teachers, and Parents:

Blastoff! Readers are carefully developed by literacy experts and combine standards-based content with developmentally appropriate text.

Level 1 provides the most support through repetition of high-frequency words, light text, predictable sentence patterns, and strong visual support.

Level 2 offers early readers a bit more challenge through varied simple sentences, increased text load, and less repetition of high-frequency words.

Level 3 advances early-fluent readers toward fluency through increased text and concept load, less reliance on visuals, longer sentences, and more literary language.

Level 4 builds reading stamina by providing more text per page, increased use of punctuation, greater variation in sentence patterns, and increasingly challenging vocabulary.

Level 5 encourages children to move from "learning to read" to "reading to learn" by providing even more text, varied writing styles, and less familiar topics.

Whichever book is right for your reader, Blastoff! Readers are the perfect books to build confidence and encourage a love of reading that will last a lifetime!

This edition first published in 2014 by Bellwether Media, Inc.

No part of this publication may be reproduced in whole or in part without written permission of the publisher. For information regarding permission, write to Bellwether Media, Inc., Attention: Permissions Department, 5357 Penn Avenue South, Minneapolis, MN 55419.

Library of Congress Cataloging-in-Publication Data

Ryan, Patrick, 1948-
Iowa / by Pat Ryan.
    pages cm. – (Blastoff! readers. Exploring the states)
Includes bibliographical references and index.
Summary: "Developed by literacy experts for students in grades three through seven, this book introduces young readers to the geography and culture of Iowa"– Provided by publisher.
ISBN 978-1-62617-014-8 (hardcover : alk. paper)
1. Iowa–Juvenile literature. I. Title.
F621.3.R93 2014
977.7–dc23
                                                      2013004893

Printed in the United States of America, North Mankato, MN.

Table of Contents

Where Is Iowa?

South Dakota

N
W E
S

Sioux City

Nebraska

Missouri River

Iowa covers 56,273 square miles (145,746 square kilometers) in the **Midwest** region of the United States. The rectangular state sits between two major rivers. The Missouri River follows its western border. The Mississippi River forms the eastern edge.

Minnesota

Wisconsin

Iowa

Mississippi River

Cedar Rapids

Iowa City

Davenport

Des Moines

Missouri

Illinois

Wisconsin and Illinois are Iowa's eastern neighbors. The state's western border meets South Dakota and Nebraska. Minnesota is to the north and Missouri is to the south. The capital city of Des Moines lies near the center of Iowa. It is the state's biggest city.

History

Native Americans first lived off the land that is Iowa. They hunted bison and planted corn. European explorers claimed the land for France in the late 1600s. In 1803, France sold Iowa to the United States under the **Louisiana Purchase**. Over time, the U.S. government pushed Native Americans out of Iowa. In 1846, Iowa became the twenty-ninth state.

Did you know?
The Sauk and Fox tribes fought to keep their land in the Black Hawk War. However, they lost to the United States.

Black Hawk War

Iowa Timeline!

1673: French explorers Jacques Marquette and Louis Joliet find Iowa on their way down the Mississippi River.

1803: The U.S. gains Iowa as part of the Louisiana Purchase. Lewis and Clark explore the area the next year.

1832: Native Americans lose their land in the Black Hawk War.

1846: Iowa becomes the twenty-ninth state.

1867: The Chicago, Iowa and Nebraska Railroad becomes the first to cross the state.

1928: Iowa native Herbert Hoover becomes the thirty-first President of the United States.

1930s: Many poor Iowa farmers lose their land during the Great Depression.

1993: The Great Flood destroys cities and farms across the state.

Jacques Marquette and Louis Joliet

Herbert Hoover

The Great Flood of 1993

The Land

Did you know?
The highest point in Iowa is near the Minnesota border. It is named Hawkeye Point after the famous Sauk chief named Black Hawk.

Mississippi River bluffs

Rolling hills and **plains** make up most of Iowa's **fertile** landscape. The flat land is the result of **glaciers**. These ice sheets pressed the land during the Ice Age. **Bluffs** line the eastern and western edges of the state.

Iowa's Climate

average °F

spring
Low: 38°
High: 59°

summer
Low: 61°
High: 83°

fall
Low: 40°
High: 61°

winter
Low: 13°
High: 31°

Iowa has three main land areas. The Young **Drift** Plains stretch across the northern and central parts of the state. They contain a lot of loose ground, or drift. Hills and cliffs fill the Driftless Area in the northeast. The Dissected Till Plains roll across the southern part of the state. Rivers and streams cut into the land to shape these plains.

Loess Hills

Western Iowa is home to a rolling landscape called the **Loess** Hills. The region is covered with yellowish loess. This is loose soil carried by the wind. About 25,000 years ago, melting glaciers in the northern United States left behind tiny grains of **silt**. Wind swept up the silt and dropped it along the Missouri River. Over time, this process formed layered hills.

The Loess Hills are delicate. They **erode** easily and have sharp ridges as a result. Still, much of the region is used for farming because loess is rich soil. Prairie grasses, wildflowers, and bur oaks blanket the preserved areas and attract hikers to the hills.

Loess Hills

Iowa

N
W E
S

Wildlife

pheasant

white-tailed deer

bull snake

Iowa is home to **hardy** animals that can adapt to weather changes. Bison, elk, and other large animals roamed the plains before farms and trains appeared. Today, white-tailed deer and smaller mammals are more common.

bald eagle

Did you know?
Many animals disappeared from Iowa when forests became farmland. People are working hard to protect the habitats that remain for endangered animals.

Timber rattlesnakes and bull snakes slither across prairies. Bluebirds, cardinals, and other small birds populate Iowa's tree branches. **Game** birds include pheasants, quail, and wild turkeys. The white heads of bald eagles can be spotted in the trees alongside rivers. Bass, pike, and other fish swim underwater.

Landmarks

Iowa has a collection of landmarks that show off its history and people. The Herbert Hoover National Historic Site in West Branch shows the birthplace of the thirty-first U.S. President. Visitors can see the cottage where President Hoover grew up and tour a museum about his life.

A cornfield in Dyersville is a famous Iowa site thanks to the baseball movie *Field of Dreams*. The field features a baseball diamond and farmhouse. In Pella, the tallest working Dutch windmill in America shows off the town's roots. The windmill reaches a height of 124 feet (38 meters)!

birthplace of Herbert Hoover

Dyersville cornfield

Pella's Dutch windmill

Des Moines

Des Moines is the state capital of Iowa. This city's domed **capitol** building hosts the state government. National **politicians** also gather in Des Moines for the important Iowa **caucuses**. These meetings help select U.S. presidential candidates.

Iowa State Capitol

Des Moines
Art Center

Des Moines is also a
center of culture. The
Des Moines Art Center displays world-famous art inside
its blocky structure. Other museums in the city offer a
peek at farming and Iowa's past. Des Moines is Iowa's
true center of politics, history, and art.

Farming is a major field of work in Iowa. The state has more than 90,000 farms! Iowa's farmers are among the country's top producers of beef, pork, and corn. They also grow oats, wheat, and other crops in the rich soil.

Service jobs offer work for most Iowans. Many jobs are in the **insurance** business. People also work for banks, schools, and the government. Factory workers make food products and farm equipment, including John Deere tractors.

Where People Work in Iowa

manufacturing
12%

farming and
natural resources
6%

services
69%

government
13%

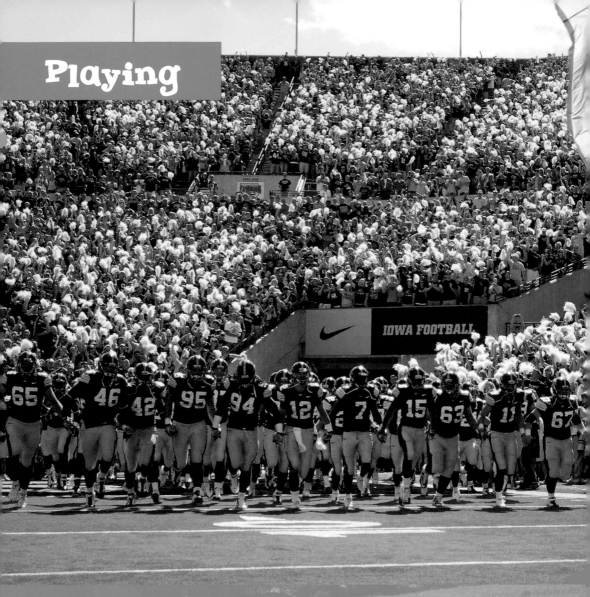

Playing

Iowans root for their college sports teams because they do not have their own professional teams. The Iowa State Cyclones and the University of Iowa Hawkeyes are state rivals. Golf is a sport many Iowans enjoy playing. The flat landscapes across the state make perfect grounds for golf courses.

Iowans also get outside for outdoor fun. Bike trails wind around the state for those who love to pedal. Kids in Iowa weave through giant corn mazes for fun at some farms. In open and wooded areas, hunters track small game animals. Boaters take to Iowa's waters to fish, relax, and water-ski.

Tater Tot Casserole

Ingredients:

- 1 1/2 lbs ground beef
- 1 bag tater tots
- 1 can condensed cream of mushroom soup
- 1 can condensed cream of celery soup
- 1 can green beans, drained
- 1 can corn, drained
- 1 1/2 cups shredded cheddar cheese (optional)
- 1/2 teaspoon salt
- 1/2 teaspoon pepper

Directions:

1. Preheat oven to 350°F.

2. Brown beef, drain.

3. Mix browned beef, salt, pepper, soup, corn, and green beans. Pour in casserole dish.

4. Place tater tots in lines on top of beef mixture so entire top is covered. Top with cheese, if desired.

5. Cover with foil and bake 45 minutes. Remove foil and bake 15 minutes. Serve immediately.

pork tenderloin sandwich

Iowans are known for their comfort food. Casseroles feed people at family gatherings and community events. The casseroles often include beef or pork, mixed vegetables, and noodles. Sometimes they are topped with tater tots.

Iowans load their plates with farm-fresh food. A common dinner is meat with potatoes and other vegetables. Sweet corn is a favorite vegetable. The pork tenderloin sandwich is one of the most popular sandwiches in Iowa. This is breaded pork that is deep-fried and put on a bun.

Tulip Time Festival

The State Fair is a major Iowa gathering every August. People sample a variety of fair foods while they watch livestock shows or concerts. Adventurous fairgoers enjoy fast spinning rides. The National Balloon Classic also takes place in late summer. More than 100 hot air balloons color the sky in Indianola.

National Balloon Classic

RAGBRAI

! fun fact

RAGBRAI riders dip their back bike wheels into the Missouri River before they begin pedaling. At the end of the ride, they place their front wheels in the Mississippi River.

Bicyclists make their way to Iowa in July to pedal in the Register's Annual Great Bicycle Ride Across Iowa (RAGBRAI). This week-long bike ride winds through the state. In May, people crowd into Pella for the Tulip Time Festival. Beautiful tulips color the town as people celebrate its Dutch heritage.

The Amana Colonies

Did you know?
The word *Amana* means "believe faithfully." It was a fitting name for colonies united by deep faith.

AMANA COLONIES ANTIQUES

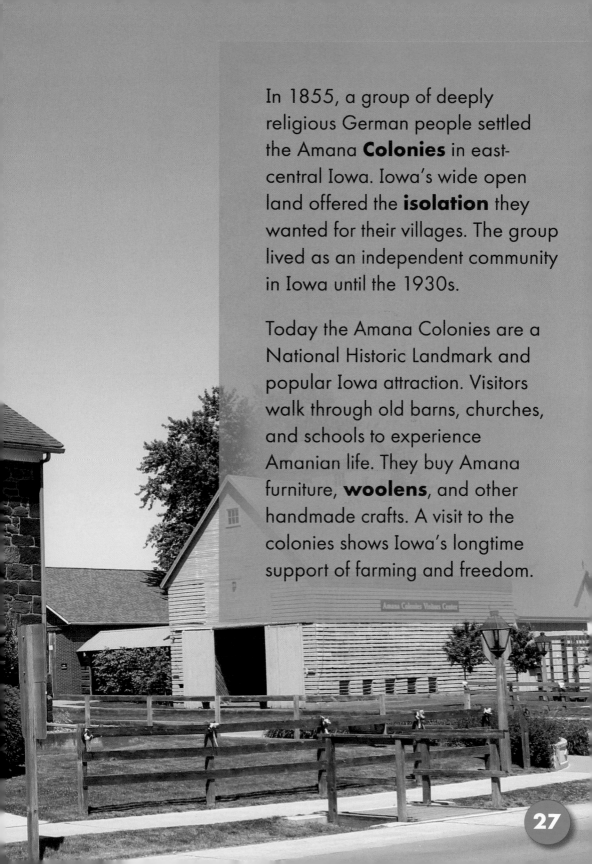

In 1855, a group of deeply religious German people settled the Amana **Colonies** in east-central Iowa. Iowa's wide open land offered the **isolation** they wanted for their villages. The group lived as an independent community in Iowa until the 1930s.

Today the Amana Colonies are a National Historic Landmark and popular Iowa attraction. Visitors walk through old barns, churches, and schools to experience Amanian life. They buy Amana furniture, **woolens**, and other handmade crafts. A visit to the colonies shows Iowa's longtime support of farming and freedom.

Fast Facts About Iowa

Iowa's Flag

Iowa's flag has three vertical stripes. The thick, white stripe in the center stands for purity. The blue one on the left represents loyalty. The red stripe on the right is for courage. In the center, a bald eagle holds a ribbon with the state motto.

State Flower
wild prairie rose

State Nicknames:	Hawkeye State Tall Corn State
State Motto:	"Our Liberties We Prize and Our Rights We Will Maintain"
Year of Statehood:	1846
Capital City:	Des Moines
Other Major Cities:	Cedar Rapids, Davenport, Iowa City, Sioux City
Population:	3,046,355 (2010)
Area:	56,273 square miles (145,746 square kilometers); Iowa is the 26th largest state.
Major Industries:	farming, food production, insurance, services, manufacturing
Natural Resources:	farmland, limestone, cement
State Government:	100 representatives; 50 senators
Federal Government:	4 representatives; 2 senators
Electoral Votes:	6

State Bird
eastern goldfinch

Glossary

bluffs—cliffs or steep banks

capitol—the building in which state representatives and senators meet

caucuses—meetings in which members of a political party choose candidates to represent the group

colonies—territories owned and settled by people from another country

drift—scattered loose ground moved by glaciers; clay and sand are examples of drift.

erode—to wear away due to moving wind, water, or glaciers

fertile—able to support growth

game—wild animals hunted for food or sport

glaciers—massive sheets of ice that cover large areas of land

hardy—able to bear harsh and changing conditions

insurance—the paying of regular sums of money for protection in the case of damage or illness

isolation—being removed and set apart from other people

loess—soil that has been carried by the wind and deposited somewhere else

Louisiana Purchase—a deal made between France and the United States; it gave the United States 828,000 square miles (2,144,510 square kilometers) of land west of the Mississippi River.

Midwest—a region of 12 states in the north-central United States

native—originally from a specific place

plains—large areas of flat land

politicians—government representatives who make laws

service jobs—jobs that perform tasks for people or businesses

silt—soil carried by moving water

woolens—clothing and other items made with wool

To Learn More

AT THE LIBRARY

Freedman, Jeri. *Iowa: Past and Present*. New York, N.Y.: Rosen Central, 2010.

Murray, Julie. *Iowa*. Minneapolis, Minn.: ABDO Pub. Co., 2013.

Nielsen, L. Michelle. *The Biography of Corn*. New York, N.Y.: Crabtree Pub. Co., 2007.

ON THE WEB

Learning more about Iowa is as easy as 1, 2, 3.

1. Go to www.factsurfer.com.

2. Enter "Iowa" into the search box.

3. Click the "Surf" button and you will see a list of related Web sites.

With factsurfer.com, finding more information is just a click away.

Index

The images in this book are reproduced through the courtesy of: Agstockusa/ Age Fotostock, front cover (bottom), p. 18; North Wind Picture Archives/ Alamy, p. 6; (Collection)/ Prints & Photographs Division/ Library of Congress, p. 7 (left); Elmer Wesley Greene/ Wikipedia, p. 7 (middle); AP Photo/ Charlie Neibergall/ Associated Press, p. 7 (right); Gary Randall/ Kimball Stock, p. 8; Larry Lindell, pp. 8-9; Tom Bean/ Corbis/ Glow Images, pp. 10-11; Costas Anton Dumitrescu, p. 12 (top); James Marvin Phelps, p. 12 (middle); Joe Farah, p. 12 (bottom); David & Micha Sheldon/ F1 online/ Glow Images, pp. 12-13; Andre Jenny Stock Connection Worldwide/ Newscom, p. 14 (top); Phil Velasquez KRT/ Newscom, p. 14 (bottom); Don Smetzer/ Alamy, pp. 14-15; Denis Jr. Tangney, pp. 16-17; Tim Abramowitz, p. 17 (top); Walter Bibikow/ Getty Images, p. 17 (bottom); Imagebroker/ Alamy, p. 19; Louis Brems/ SCG/ Zuma Press.com/ Newscom, pp. 20-21; Fredricksburg, Iowa, USA/ Alamy, p. 21; Andrea Skjold, p. 22; Nitr, p. 23 (top); Charles Brutlag, p. 23 (bottom); Elaine McDonald, pp. 24-25; Michael Rolands, p. 25 (top); AP Photo/ The Telegraph Herald, Mike Burley/ Associated Press, p. 25 (bottom); Dustin88, pp. 26-27; Trubach, p. 28 (top); Jay Stuhlmiller, p. 28 (bottom); Brandon Alms, p. 29.